THIS BOOK BELONGS TO:

....

....

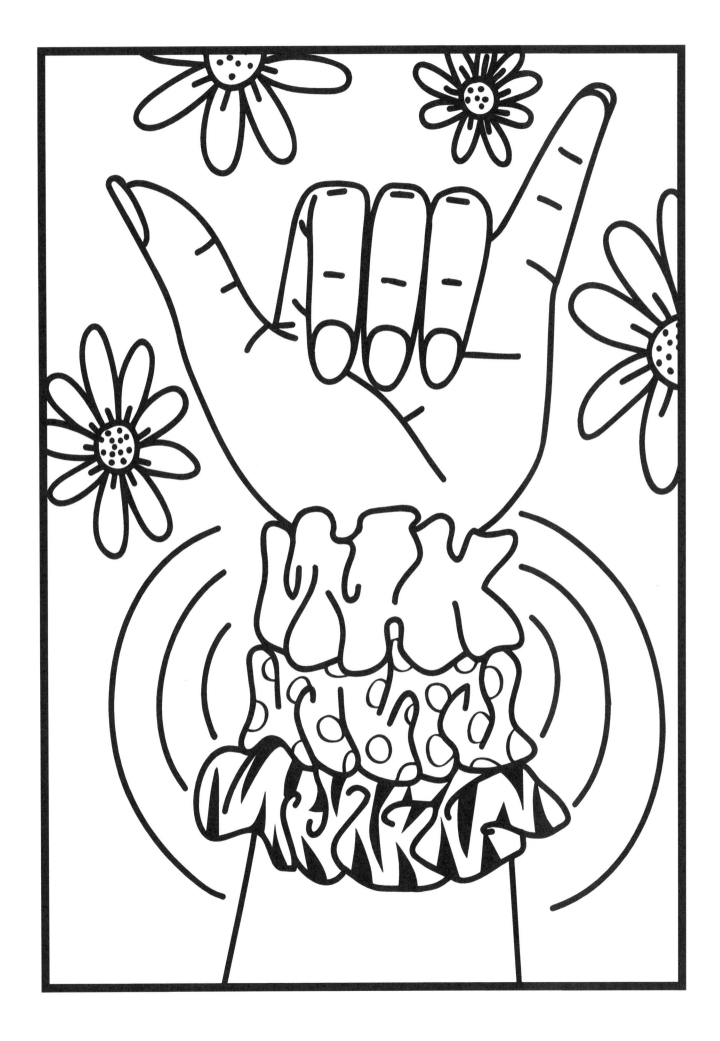

FIRST OF ALL, THANK YOU FOR PURCHASING THIS BOOK
I HOPE THAT IT ADDED AT VALUE AND QUALITY TO YOUR EVERYDAY LIFE.
IF SO, IT WOULD BE REALLY NICE IF YOU COULD
TAKE SOME TIME TO POST A REVIEW ON AMAZON.

YOUR FEEDBACK WILL BE HIGHLY APPRECIATED!

SCAN ME

Made in United States
Troutdale, OR
12/06/2024

25981060R00060